D0646413

Family
and
Friends

BY KATHY THORNBOROUGH • ILLUSTRATIONS BY KATHLEEN PETELINSEK

The Child's World®

A SPECIAL THANKS TO OUR ADVISERS:

As a member of a deaf family that spans four generations, Kim Bianco Majeri lives, works, and plays amongst the deaf community.

Carmine L. Vozzolo is an educator of children who are deaf and hard of hearing, as well as their families.

PUBLISHED by The Child's World®
1980 Lookout Drive • Mankato, MN 56003-1705
800-599-READ • www.childsworld.com

ACKNOWLEDGMENTS
The Child's World®: Mary Berendes, Publishing Director
The Design Lab: Design
Jody Jensen Shaffer: Editing

PHOTO CREDITS
© andresrimaging/iStock.com: 3; Aletia/Shutterstock.com: 18-19;
DaydreamsGirl/iStock.com: 22; grandriver/iStock.com: 14; Irina
Schmidt/Shutterstock.com: 11; lightwavemedia/Shutterstock.com:
back cover, 21; Levent Konuk/Shutterstock.com: 5; lisafx/iStock.
com: 13; lostinbids/iStock.com: back cover, 10; Martinan/iStock.
com: 17; monkeybusinessimages/iStock.com: 12; moxiegirl12/
iStock.com: 23; PetrMalyshev/iStock.com: 15; sirikorn thamniyom/
Shutterstock.com: cover, 1, 16; sonyae/iStock.com: 8-9;
Studio1One/iStock.com: 6; Syda Productions/Shutterstock.com: 4;
Vanessa Nel/Shutterstock.com: 7; ZouZou/Shutterstock.com: 20

ISBN 9781626873179
LCCN 2014934490

PRINTED in the United States of America
Mankato, MN
July, 2014
PA02216

NOTE TO PARENTS AND EDUCATORS:

The understanding of any language begins with the acquisition of vocabulary, whether the language is spoken or manual. The books in the Talking Hands series provide readers, both young and old, with a first introduction to basic American Sign Language signs. Combining close photocues and simple, but detailed, line illustrations, children and adults alike can begin the process of learning American Sign Language. Let these books be an introduction to the world of American Sign Language. Most languages have regional dialects and multiple ways of expressing the same thought. This is also true for sign language. We have attempted to use the most common version of the signs for the words in this series. As with any language, the best way to learn is to be taught in person by a frequent user. It is our hope that this series will pique your interest in sign language.

A family can have lots of different members.

Family

Make the "F" sign with both hands facing each other. Then roll your wrists so that your pinkies touch.

3

Mother

Tap your chin twice
with your thumb.

Some people call
their mothers "Mom,"
"Mommy," or "Mama."

Father

Tap your forehead twice
with your thumb.

Some people call
their fathers "Dad,"
"Daddy," or "Papa."

Son

In Spanish, "son" is *hijo* (EE-ho).

Start with your right hand in a salute.
Move your hand down to end
as if you are holding a baby.

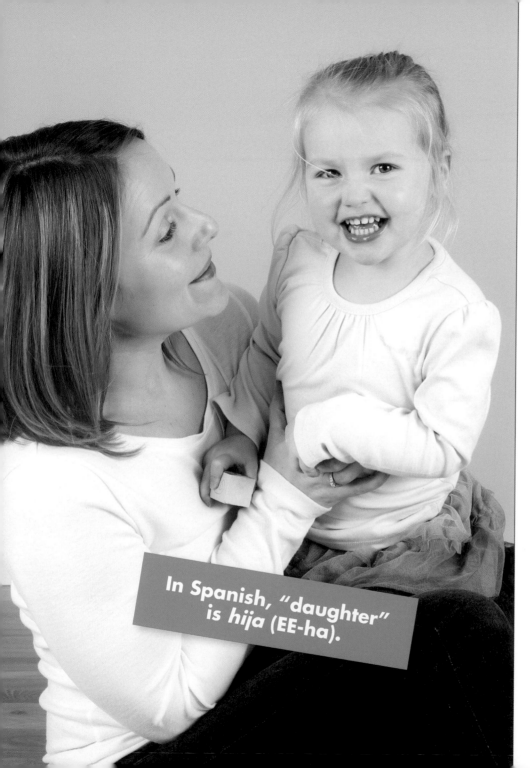

In Spanish, "daughter" is *hija* (EE-ha).

Daughter

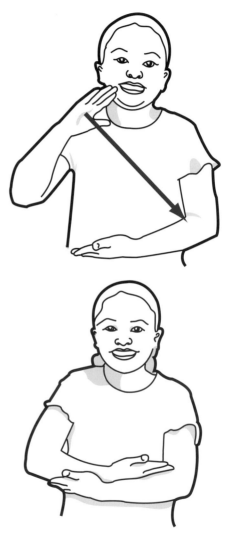

Start with your right hand touching your chin. Move your hand down to end as if you are holding a baby.

Brother

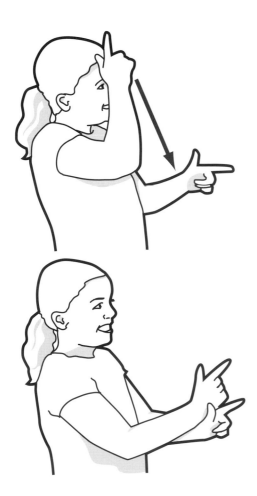

Both hands make the "L" sign.
Touch your right hand to your forehead,
then move down until your right wrist
rests on your left.

Two famous brothers were the Wright Brothers. They flew the first airplane.

Sister

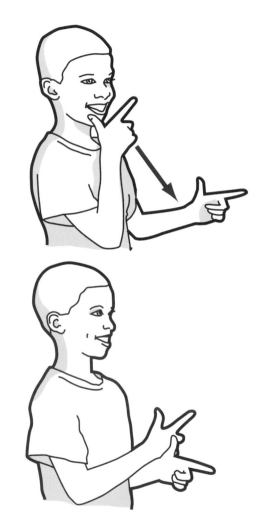

Two famous sisters are Venus and Serena Williams. They are tennis champions.

Both hands make the "L" sign. Touch your right hand to your chin, then move down until your right wrist rests on your left.

Baby

Babies cannot talk at first. They must cry to communicate.

Swing your arms back and forth as if you were rocking a baby.

Child

Motion your hand downward twice.
Pretend as if you are patting a child
on the head.

A child who is between
one and three years old is
often called a "toddler."

Children

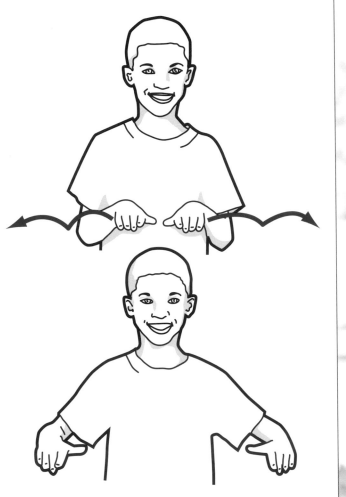

Move hands downward and out,
as if you were patting more
than one child on the head.

Aunt

Make the "A" sign with your right hand.
Twist your wrist a few times
near your cheek.

**Your aunt is the sister of
either your mom or dad.**

13

Uncle

Make the "U" sign with your right hand. Hold your hand close to your right temple and twist your wrist a few times.

Your uncle is the brother of either your mom or dad.

Your cousin is the child of your uncle or aunt.

Cousin

Make the "C" sign with your right hand. Shake or twist your wrist near your cheek.

Grandmother

Touch your thumb to your chin.
Bounce your hand outward twice.

Some people call their grandmothers "Grandma," "Nana," or "Abuela."

Some people call their grandfathers "Grandpa," "Papa," or "Abuelo."

Grandfather

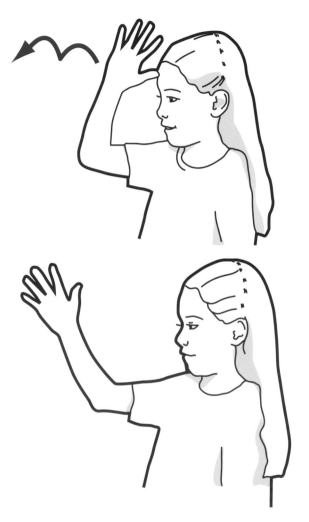

Touch your thumb to your firehead.
Bounce your hand outward twice.

17

Nephew

Make the "N" sign with your right hand. Twist your wrist near your right eye.

A nephew is the son of someone's brother or sister.

Niece

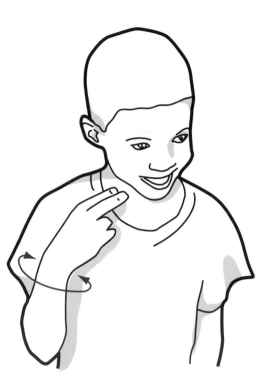

Make the "N" sign with your
right hand. Twist your wrist
near your right jaw.

Parent

Touch your thumb to your chin.
Then quickly touch your thumb
to your forehead.

Many people look like their parents.

Husband

A man getting married is called a groom.

With your right hand, make the "C" sign near your forehead. Then move your hand down into your left hand.

Wife

With your right hand, make the "C" sign near your chin. Then move your hand down into your left hand.

A woman getting married is called a bride.

Having a friend can make you feel happy.

Friend

Twist your index fingers together with your right finger on top. Take them apart and put them back together—this time with the left finger on top.

23

A SPECIAL THANK YOU!

A special thank you to our models from the Program for Children Who are Deaf and Hard of Hearing at the Alexander Graham Bell Elementary School in Chicago, Illinois.

Alina's favorite things to do are art, soccer, and swimming. DJ is her brother!

Dareous likes football. His favorite team is the Detroit Lions. He also likes to play video games.

Darionna likes the swings and merry-go-round on the playground. She also loves art.

DJ loves playing the harmonica and video games. Alina is his sister!

Jasmine likes writing and math in school. She also loves to swim.